EXPLORING THE FREMONT

DAVID B. MADSEN
FOREWORD, TERRY TEMPEST WILLIAMS

UTAH MUSEUM OF NATURAL HISTORY
UNIVERSITY OF UTAH

Front cover: Ivie Creek black-on-white vessel from
Pharo Village (42Md180 fs206.1)

Photographs by John Telford
Design by IMS Graphics Services/James S. Omer
Illustrations by James S. Omer
Typography by Twin Typographers
Printing by University Printing Services
Printed on Paloma Coated Matte Basis 80
Cover printed on Curtis Flannel Cover Basis 80
Typeface: Novarese

University of Utah Occasional Publication Number Eight

Library of Congress Catalog Card Number: 89-52038

ISBN Number: 0-940378-35-3

THIS PUBLICATION IS PRODUCED
IN COOPERATION WITH
THE UTAH DIVISION OF STATE HISTORY
AND SUPPORTED BY
A GENEROUS GRANT FROM
THE R. HAROLD BURTON FOUNDATION.

PREFACE AND ACKNOWLEDGE-MENTS

With publication of *Exploring the Fremont*, the Utah Museum of Natural History is pleased to present the eighth volume in its Occasional Publications Series. The work is an adjunct to the exhibit of the same name, and is the Museum's first exhibit catalog; it will also serve as a continuing reference about this important prehistoric group. The Utah Museum of Natural History holds, as a public trust and for the future, a large archaeological collection that has been built by a century of University of Utah scholarship. The collection is regularly used for research; with this publication the Museum shares pieces of it with the public. All of the wonderful objects illustrated here are in the Utah Museum of Natural History, unless otherwise noted.

We gratefully acknowledge the contributions of the many people and agencies who helped make this book possible: the R. Harold Burton Foundation; the Utah Division of State History; the University of Utah Archaeological Center; University of Utah IMS Graphics and Photographic Services; University Printing Services; the Emery County Museum; the Office of Public Archaeology at Brigham Young University; the Peabody Museum at Harvard University; the Anthropological Archives at the Smithsonian Institution; Eldon J. Dorman; the multi-talented James S. Omer; John Telford, whose brilliant photographs add weight and texture to these printed pages; Terry Tempest Williams, Museum Naturalist-in-Residence, and other members of the Museum staff, including Development Director Nancy Devenport; and Assistant Curator of Collections Laurel Casjens, whose meticulous work is represented in captions and photo selection and credits. Finally, we honor David B. Madsen, for his scholarship, his care, his vision.

Donald V. Hague   Ann Hanniball
Director   *Project Director*

Any work like this can only be produced with the aid of a large number of people, and, while I cannot hope to identify them all here, I do want everyone involved to know how much I appreciate their help. There are five, however, without whom the piece would never been started and, most certainly, never have been finished, who must be singled out for their contributions.

Donald V. Hague, Director of the Utah Museum of Natural History, conceived of a special exhibit on the Fremont and was the prime mover behind its design and execution. The form and structure of the exhibit, held October 13, 1989 through March 4, 1990, served as the basis for this volume.

Ann Hanniball, Curator of Collections at the Museum, is without a doubt the person most responsible for producing the work. It was, first of all, her idea; second, she is the one who convinced all the contributors that it was worth the effort; third, she graciously assumed the responsibility for all phases of production, from selecting paper stock to determining layout; fourth, she reviewed four or five different versions of the manuscript until she got the one she wanted; and fifth and perhaps most importantly, she helped raise the funds which made it all possible. The volume is hers more than anyone's.

Terry Tempest Williams' skillful editing gave form and substance to my often turgid prose. Without her ability to see and extract meaning from an obtuse and obscure manuscript and to communicate meaning to a general audience, this volume would be much less than it is.

Laurel Casjens, Assistant Curator of Collections at the Museum, helped select, arrange and photograph the artifacts included here and helped reproduce the many original site photographs and maps. She also reviewed the manuscript and did most of the actual leg-work in producing the volume.

James S. Omer, Graphic Artist, Instructional Media Services, designed the book, produced all of the line drawings included here, and supervised the layout. He made it look good.

The institutional support provided by the Utah Museum of Natural History and the Utah Division of State History made this work possible, but it was the gracious contribution of the R. Harold Burton Foundation to the Museum which ultimately enabled the work to proceed.

David B. Madsen

CONTENTS

FOREWORD

Think about a people who made clay figurines with shuttered eyes, staring at us from a distant past and then think about the Fremont. They inhabited the eastern Great Basin and western Colorado Plateau from approximately 650 to 1250 A.D., roughly a thousand years ago. They planted corn, irrigated their fields, and utilized wild foods with ingenuity. In many ways, the Fremont correspond with the Anasazi. But in many ways, they do not.

The Anasazi were a group of people with a complex social organization: clans, elaborate kivas and road systems. In contrast, the Fremont were small bands of people, much more closely tied to their immediate environment. They were flexible, adaptive, and diverse.

Some archaeologists believe the Fremont developed out of the existing groups of hunters and gatherers of this region. Fremont people varied from large sedentary populations, villages, to highly mobile clans. An austere rock shelter above the salt flats; a verdant marsh on the edge of Utah Lake; or aspen hillsides in Salina Canyon—all house the spirit of the Fremont.

So does the Utah Museum of Natural History. Thousands of objects associated with Fremont culture are cataloged and stored here. It is a diverse collection of artifacts ranging from soil samples taken from particular sites to basketry, pottery, moccasins, and clay figurines. Some of the objects take your breath away. But as museum professionals, we are trained to keep our distance, not to be moved by inanimate things. The curation of any museum collection is a science, rational and orderly, meticulous and thorough. We preserve the past for the future. Human contact is restricted to the wearing of white cotton gloves and lab coats. Lights are low. Room temperatures are checked. Each object is numbered. Site recognition is immediate. Any object can be recalled and detailed on the Museum's computerized database known as "MIMS" (museum inventory and management system). It is a controlled environment.

But sometimes the objects run away with you. They seize your

Figure 1 Clay figurine from the Grantsville Mounds (11173)

imagination and begin to sing songs of another day when bone whistles called blue-winged teals down to the marshes at Bear River. You hear them. You turn around. You are alone. It is always this way. Suddenly, the single glove made of deer hide moves and you see a cold hand shivering inside Promontory Cave. It waves from the distance of a thousand years.

And sometimes you recognize images from your own experience. I recall looking at a Great Salt Lake gray variant potsherd. A design had been pecked on its surface. It was infinitely familiar and then it came to me—shorebirds standing in water, long-legged birds, the dazzling light reflected on feathers. I had seen it a million times on the shores of Great Salt Lake—godwits, curlews, avocets, and stilts—birds the Fremont knew well. Their lives depended on them.

These are leaps of the imagination, I know, but of what value are objects of a past people if we don't allow ourselves to be touched by them. They are alive. They have a voice. They remind us what it means to be human; that it is our nature to survive, to be resourceful, to be attentive to the world we live in. A necklace of olivella shells worn by a Fremont man or woman celebrates our instinctive desire for beauty, even power and prestige. A polished stone ball, horned figurines, incised bones and stone tablets court the mysteries of private lives, communal lives, lives rooted in ritual and ceremony. In the end, we are left with more questions than answers. What we do know is that the Fremont were a people of place and the homeland of the Fremont lies in Utah.

Stansbury Island is a sacred place to me. It is a stark and severe landscape. The light is searing. Temperatures are extreme. Great Salt Lake mirrors the sky as waves hiss each time they fold on to the beach. And it is lovely. I walk this country often. What I have learned over the years is that the Fremont walked here, too.

One night, a full moon watched over me like a mother. In the blue light of the basin, I saw a petroglyph on a large boulder. It was a spiral. I placed the tip of my finger on the center and began tracing the coil

x

around and around. It spun off the rock. My finger kept circling the land, the lake, the sky. The spiral became larger and larger until it became a dance of stars in the night sky above Stansbury Island. A meteor flashed and as quickly disappeared. The waves continued to hiss and retreat, hiss and retreat. In the West Desert of the Great Basin, I was not alone.

Terry Tempest Williams
Naturalist-in-Residence
Utah Museum of Natural History

Figure 2 Great Salt Lake gray variant potsherd (42Bo55 fs10.1)

The Fremont have always mystified me.

As an anthropologist, my basic interest is to know why people do what they do. I am also an archaeologist because one of the best ways to determine patterns of behavior and their cause is by investigating the material remains of behavior repeated over scores of generations.

The Fremont should be an excellent subject for an anthropological archaeologist to study. They are relatively recent and many of their sites are so well preserved that we are as likely to know as much about them as about any prehistoric society. Yet they seem to defy categorization.

I have studied the Fremont for more than twenty years, but the more I learn about them the less I seem to understand. Just when I and other archaeologists think we have a good way of defining Fremont variations, something new crops up that does not seem to fit. Patterns seem to float just out of reach. Exactly why this is so is not yet clear to me, and until it is I will remain fascinated by the Fremont.

It is clear that the problem is with the way we do archaeology, not with the Fremont themselves. They are no more enigmatic than any other human society. Most of us tend to see the Fremont and many other prehistoric societies in terms of extremes; either as ignorant savages blundering their way through life or as primitive spiritualists living in harmony with nature and the world around them. But the Fremont were just like every human group; some were cruel and some were benevolent; some were smart and some were a little slow; some worked hard and some were lazy. They were human beings, simply that, trying to raise children in a variable and sometimes harsh landscape.

We have much to learn as we explore the Fremont. They were people like you and me. By understanding them, we can better understand ourselves and how we come to a sense of place in the Desert West.

Figure 3 Chipped stone drills were probably used in the construction of other tools and equipment, such as making repair holes in cracked ceramic vessels. (top: 42In124 fs175.70, bottom: 42In124 fs237.23)

xiii

Rock art, painted design in
Clear Creek Canyon, Utah

West of the Rockies and east of the Sierra Nevada is a landscape that beckons the imagination yet defies easy description. Unlike the grasslands of the Plains, the deserts of the Southwest, or the hardwood forests of the Southeast, it is a landscape impossible to evoke in a single word or phrase. It is a land of variation and diversity; no one

A FREMONT SYNOPSIS

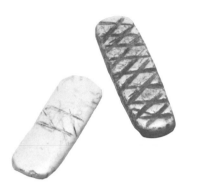

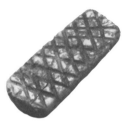

environment dominates. High alpine meadows, stark salt flats, deep slickrock canyons, broad terminal river marshes, numerous canyon streams and dry pinyon/juniper forests are all found within a few hours drive of each other. Variation is found even within these environmental categories, with small spring-fed marshes dotted through the salt flats and willow and cottonwood dominated stream-side vegetation meandering through the pinyon and juniper.

Today, with our fossil fuels and complex technology, we can temper this diversity and impose a social and cultural uniformity that is only loosely linked to the landscape in which we live. A thousand years ago, however, such a separation between environment and culture was not possible, and the people who lived here before us were more closely tied to the land.

Like the land, the prehistoric societies of the western Colorado Plateau and the eastern Great Basin can also be characterized by variation and diversity and are neither readily defined nor easily encapsulated within a single description. Some people were primarily settled farmers, growing corn, beans, and squash in small plots along streams at the base of mountain ranges; some were nomads, collecting wild plants and animals to support themselves; still others would shift between these lifestyles. In some areas the population was relatively dense, in others only small groups were found widely scattered across the landscape. People living in this region may even have spoken different languages or had widely divergent dialects. Yet, despite the diversity of these lifestyles and the varied geography which structured their actions, these people seem to have shared patterns of behavior and ways of living which tie them together.

Today we call these scattered groups of hunters and farmers the Fremont, but that name may be more reflective of our own need to categorize things than it is a reflection of how closely related these people were. "Fremont" is really a generic label for a people who, like the land in which they lived, are not easily described or classified.

Because the Fremont are not easily categorized and do not readily

fit into archaeological classification schemes, they have been a source of confusion and debate among archaeologists since they were first identified in the late 1920s. The differences between the many small bands of the Great Basin and northern Colorado Plateau areas of the Intermountain West were often quite great. As a result, archaeologists have had a difficult time defining just who these people were and how they were related to each other. There are actually very few artifact similarities among these groups. While these include such things as a particular way of making baskets, a unique moccasin style, clay figurines, and gray pottery, the problem of categorizing Fremont groups is compounded by a number of factors. The figurines are quite rare, for example, and the baskets and moccasins are perishable materials which do not survive in most archaeological sites. There is, in fact, only a single non-perishable trait which ties these people together. That single feature is a thin-walled gray pottery whose many variations have been found west to Ely and Elko, Nevada in the central Great Basin, north to Pocatello, Idaho on the Snake River Plain, east to Grand Junction, Colorado and the foot of the western Rocky Mountains, and south to Moab and St. George, Utah along the Colorado and Virgin Rivers. If you stumble on an archaeological site anywhere within this region and find sherds of this distinctive gray pottery, you have found the remains of what we have come to call the Fremont.

Despite our inability to conclusively define these diverse groups as a culture, during the last seventy years we have learned much about when, where and how the Fremont lived. What we have learned most clearly is to expect the unexpected at Fremont sites and that variation is the key word in describing them. This is as true now as it was when the Fremont were first identified and recent archaeological research has generated almost as much surprise as did the early explorations.

Most archaeologists believe the Fremont developed out of existing groups of hunter-gatherers on the Colorado Plateau and in the eastern Great Basin. These small groups were, like their Fremont

Figure 4 Small, flat, rectangular pieces of worked and polished bone, often stained with red pigment and etched on one or both sides, are common in Fremont sites. They are thought to be gaming pieces. (left top to bottom: 42Un95 fs203.2, 42Sv5 AR2114, 42Un95 fs79.3, 42Jb2 fs617.21, right top to bottom: 42Un95 fs286.3, 42In40 fs94.35, 42Un95 fs203.1)

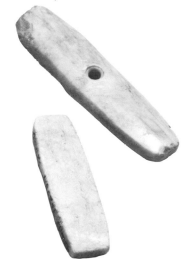

3

Figure 5 Plain gray wide-mouthed jars and narrow-necked jugs with strap handles are common utilitarian vessel forms at Fremont sites. They were often decorated by "coffee-bean" applique around the neck of the pot. Five different uniform Fremont pottery types have been defined on the basis of differences in temper, but it appears that many local wares were also produced. Uinta gray vessel (42Un95 fs36.5)

Figure 6 Sevier gray vessel (AR2079)

descendants, diverse, flexible and adaptable. They ranged from fairly large and relatively sedentary populations in environments where resources were closely spaced, to small, highly mobile family-sized groups where resources were widely dispersed. Over a span of about a thousand years, from sometime after 2500 years ago to about 1500 years ago, different groups of these hunter-gatherers gradually adopted, in a piece-meal fashion, many of the traits associated with the farming societies of the Southwest and Mexico.

First, corn and other cultivated plants (called domesticates), initially developed in what is now Mexico, diffused northward throughout

Figure 7 Trapezoidal Fremont figures may have derived from an earlier rock art style, like these Barrier Canyon style figures from the Great Gallery in Horseshoe Canyon. (Photo: Peabody Museum, Harvard University)

the greater Southwest and were added to the wild food subsistence base sometime about 2500 to 2000 years ago in areas on either side of the southern Wasatch Plateau. This early use of corn and other domesticates occurred well before settled villages developed and it seems that farming was just a part-time affair practiced by people who were still essentially nomadic hunters and gatherers. The earliest "Fremont" corn, radiocarbon dated to 2340-1940 years ago, comes from a cache near Elsinore, Utah; corn in sites along Muddy Creek in the San Rafael Swell date to just after the time of Christ. Together, these sites suggest that farming was well established in some areas by 2000 years ago. Outside this region, however, full-time hunting and gathering lifestyles seem to have continued unchanged. For example, in the deserts of the eastern Great Basin, at all of the many cave sites like Fish Springs, Lakeside, Black Rock and Danger Caves, domesticates are absent throughout this early period and subsistence was based entirely on wild foods.

Second, between about 2000 to 1500 years ago, many of the objects associated with the use of domesticates, such as pottery and large basin-shaped grinding implements, were added to the tool kit. One noteworthy factor in the appearance of Fremont pottery is that it first occurs as early as 1500 years ago in several caves and rockshelters associated with mobile hunting and gathering groups and is not found in what we think of as settled villages until several hundred years later. The production and use of these tools, in addition to the growing of corn, beans, and squash, appears to have spread to other hunting and gathering groups to the north and to both the east and west of the central Wasatch Plateau region. By about 1300 years ago, sites with corn and pottery are also found in the Uinta Basin and around the Great Salt Lake and within several hundred years after that, corn and/or pottery are present throughout the Fremont region.

Third, between about 1750 and 1250 years ago, architecture at some (but far from all) open sites changed from small, thin-walled habitation structures and subterranean storage pits, to larger

Figure 8 The sticks in these cobs from Harris Wash, south-central Utah, are thought to provide a way of roasting the corn next to a fire hearth, but they may also have been used to help keep the corn away from rodents during storage. (left: 42Ga102 fs3.1, right: 42Ga102 fs2.2)

7

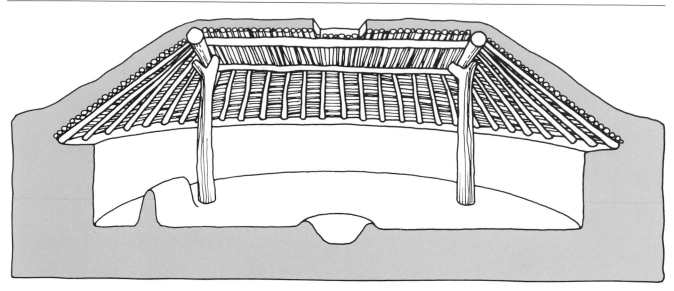

Figure 9 Artist's cut-away reconstruction of a typical Fremont pithouse

semi-subterranean timber and mud houses and above ground mud or rock walled granaries. The presence of such substantial buildings suggests that, at some sites at least, some people were becoming more fully sedentary and were relying more on farming than on collecting wild foods.

By about 750 A.D., hunting and gathering groups on the east and west sides of the Wasatch Plateau had adopted and modified many features of settled village life and to a greater or lesser extent integrated them into their subsistence and settlement patterns. For the next five hundred years or so, this crystallized Fremont pattern remained essentially unchanged in the heartland of the Fremont region, but many of its features, such as pottery, spread to groups as far away as central Nevada, southern Idaho, and northwestern Colorado/southwestern Wyoming. Whether these items were present in all these areas as the result of trade or local manufacture is presently unclear.

Significantly, there are actually very few common traits that distinguish what can be considered "classic" Fremont. Pithouse villages and farming are found over large areas of the United States about this same time and are not very useful in distinguishing the Fremont from other groups. Many artifact forms, such as projectile point styles, are also not unique to the Fremont and are not helpful in separating the Fremont from their contemporaries. A number of other material items, such as stone balls, basin-shaped metates with small secondary grinding surfaces, and elongated corner-notched arrow points, are characteristic of the Fremont, but they are either so variable from place to place, or so limited in distribution, that they are not very useful traits for distinguishing the Fremont.

Fortunately, there are four relatively distinctive artifact categories which do distinguish the Fremont, materially, from other prehistoric societies. Unfortunately, they are only rarely found together. The first major item is a one-rod-and-bundle basketry construction style so unique that it has led some to suggest that the Fremont culture can be defined on the basis of this single artifact category alone. This basketry technique is markedly different from that used by both contemporary Anasazi groups and from later historically known Numic-speaking groups such as the Ute and Shoshoni.

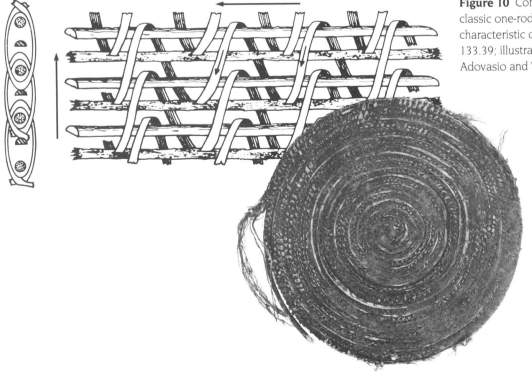

Figure 10 Construction features of the classic one-rod-and-bundle basketry characteristic of the Fremont (42Bo36 fs 133.39; illustration courtesy of J.M. Adovasio and Taraxacum Inc.)

A second trait is a unique "Fremont" moccasin style constructed from the hock of a deer or mountain sheep leg. This and other moccasin types found in Fremont sites are very different from the woven yucca sandals of the Anasazi. A third item is actually an art style represented in three dimensions by trapezoidal shaped clay figurines with readily identifiable hair "bobs" and necklaces. These same trapezoidal figures are depicted in Fremont pictographs and petroglyph panels. Magic and/or religious functions have been ascribed to these painted and sculpted figures, but no one really knows their purpose or meaning.

Figure 11 Moccasins are one of the features which distinguish the Fremont, but a number of different types were made. Some have a one piece construction with a single piece of leather pulled up around the foot. Others have a sole construction with sewn upper and lower parts. The "Fremont" type has the dew claws of a mountain sheep or deer sewn on as the heel portion of the sole. (top: 42Bo1 9764, bottom: 42Bo36 fs47.7)

Figure 12 Note the similarities in form, head, hair, and necklace between a painted clay figurine from the San Rafael Swell, and a pictograph figure from the Ashley-Dry Fork Valley. (Photos: Peabody Museum, Harvard University)

The fourth and last major artifact category is the gray coil-made pottery which is most often used to identify archaeological sites as Fremont. This pottery is not very different from that made by other Southwestern groups, and vessel forms and designs are not distinct. What distinguishes Fremont pottery from other ceramic types is the material from which it is constructed. Variations in temper, the granular rock or sand added to wet clay to insure even drying and to prevent cracking, have been used to identify five major Fremont ceramic types. They include Snake Valley gray in the southwestern part of the Fremont region, Sevier gray in the central area and Great Salt Lake gray in the northwestern area and Uinta and Emery gray in the northeast and southwestern region. Sevier, Snake Valley, and Emery gray also occur in painted varieties. A unique and beautiful painted bowl form, Ivie Creek black-on-white, is found along either side of the southern Wasatch Plateau. In addition to these five major types found at Fremont villages, a variety of locally made pottery wares are found on the fringes of the Fremont region in areas

Figure 13 Snake Valley and Sevier black-on-gray pottery is found primarily along the western margin of the Wasatch Plateau. The geometric design elements are similar to those used by the Anasazi and other Southwestern groups. Designs are usually restricted to the interiors of bowls, but occasionally painted jars were constructed.
Snake Valley black-on-gray vessels (top: 42Md180 FS349.35, bottom: 42In40 fs1209s)

occupied by people who seem to have been principally hunters and gatherers rather than farmers.

At the height of this classic Fremont period, about 1000 years ago, people who in one way or another fit the rather broad description of Fremont could be found from what is now Grand Junction, Colorado on the east to what is now Ely, Nevada on the west. They lived as far north as modern Pocatello, Idaho and on the south to present day Cedar City, Utah. Depending on what criteria are used, it is possible to divide this larger Fremont area into any number of sub-regions, and, since each new generation of archaeologists has tried to outdo the last in defining the Fremont, at least ten different distributional schemes have been produced. Presently, many archaeologists see a basic division between groups on the Colorado Plateau, usually referred to as simply the Fremont, and groups in the eastern Great Basin, often called the Sevier or Sevier-Fremont. This is primarily because the use of stone in architectural construction on the Plateau contrasts with the use of mud bricks in the Basin and because classic trapezoidal Fremont rock art figures are generally restricted to the Plateau, while the curious little portable etched stone objects common in Basin sites are not found on the Plateau. An equally useful division might be between the farming villages along the drainages on both sides of the central Wasatch Plateau and the sites outside this area which indicate a principal reliance on hunting and gathering. It is tempting to define the roughly heart-shaped area which encompasses the farming villages as the "heartland" of the Fremont, but the many hunting and gathering sites within this area suggest there is no clear-cut division; besides, Fremont archaeology hardly needs another classification scheme.

After about 1250 A.D., the Fremont, as an identifiable archaeological phenomenon, began to disappear in much the same uneven fashion that it appeared. That is, between 1250 and 1500 A.D., classic traits such as one-rod-and-bundle basketry, thin-walled gray pottery, and clay figurines disappear from the Fremont region. No one

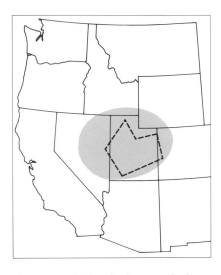

Figure 14 The hatched area is the heart of the Fremont region where settled villages are found. The shaded area represents the approximate limits of the area where Fremont pottery is recovered.

13

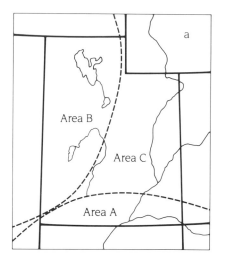

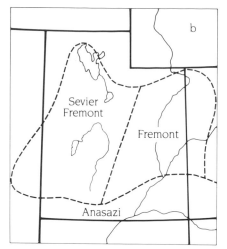

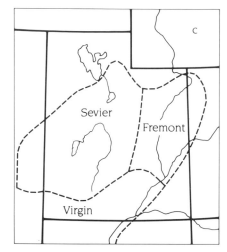

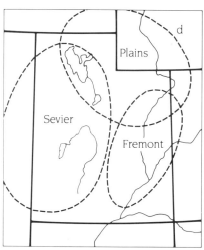

Figure 15 Various classification schemes developed by (a) Marie Wormington, 1955; (b) Jesse Jennings et al., 1956; (c) James Gunnerson, 1962; and (d) David Madsen and LaMar Lindsay, 1977

can quite agree on what happened, but there seem to be a number of interrelated factors behind this change. Two things seem most likely. First, climatic conditions favorable for farming seem to have changed during this period, forcing local groups to rely more and more on wild food resources and to adopt the increased mobility that goes along with their collection. By itself, however, this climatic change probably would not have resulted in the Fremont demise, because the flexibility and adaptability which characterized the Fremont had allowed them to weather similar changes in times past. Second, new groups of hunter-gatherers appear to have migrated into the Fremont area from the southwestern Great Basin sometime after about 1000 years ago. These full-time hunter-gatherers were apparently the ancestors of the Numic-speaking Ute, Paiute and Shoshoni peoples who inhabited the region at historic contact, and perhaps they displaced or replaced the part-time Fremont hunter-gatherers with whom they were in competition.

Whether or not Fremont peoples died out, were forced to move, or were integrated into Numic-speaking groups is unclear, and even the matter of the postulated Ute/Paiute/Shoshoni migration remains a matter of spirited debate. I, for one, think that the sudden

14

replacement of classic Fremont artifacts by different kinds of basketry, pottery, and art styles historically associated with Utah's contemporary native inhabitants, suggests that Fremont peoples were, for the most part, pushed out of the region and were replaced rather than integrated into Numic-speaking groups. This interpretation is strengthened by the fact that the most recent Fremont or Fremont-like materials, dating to about 500 years ago, are found at the northern and easternmost fringes of the Fremont region in the Douglas Creek area of northwestern Colorado and on the Snake River Plain of southern Idaho; areas at maximum distance along the postulated migration route of Numic-speaking populations.

Most archaeologists consider the Fremont to have been highly diversified hunters and gatherers living in the eastern Great Basin and western Colorado Plateau who, over a period of roughly a thousand years, gradually adopted and modified some Southwestern farming techniques and associated tool technology, and who, after another five to six hundred years of development, disappeared into immigrant populations. Unfortunately, this rather simple scenario does not tell us much about what makes Fremont people Fremont or about the variation which characterized them at any one time. More importantly, it does not really explain how and why we have come to know the Fremont in the ways that we have. Much of how we see the Fremont is a product of the way archaeology has been conducted during the last seventy years, and understanding a little of the history of Fremont archaeology is a necessary foundation to any exploration of the Fremont.

Figure 16 Finely worked bone tools were probably used as needles or perhaps for weaving. (left, top to bottom: 42Wb34 fs314.5, 42Sv6 fs646.5, 42Jb2 fs711.11, 42Bo57 fs165.19, right top to bottom: 16264, 11366.23)

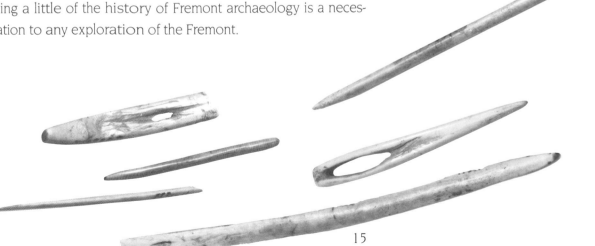

15

Rock art, Nine Mile Canyon, Utah

Archaeology is the process of trying to understand a prehistoric people by interpreting the material remains they leave behind. These material remains, such as chipped stone tools, pottery, bone scrap, collapsed buildings, and charred seeds, are related to behavioral characteristics such as language, belief systems, and marriage practices in

FREMONT ARCHAEOLOGY

Figure 17 Sketches made during excavation, such as this one from Nawthis Village, in addition to notes and photographs, provide basic data from which interpretations are made.

ways that are not yet clearly understood. Since religious or dialect differences and other similar behavioral characteristics are the principal means by which we distinguish modern groups, it is difficult to define prehistoric peoples by the relatively few physical objects left in the archaeological record. An additional problem is that these objects vary through both time and space, and organizing these continuums into understandable categories is often an archaeologist's most difficult task. Sometimes these physical remains cannot even be clearly related to human activity—coyotes and other carnivores leave many of the same kinds of broken and cracked bones in caves and rock

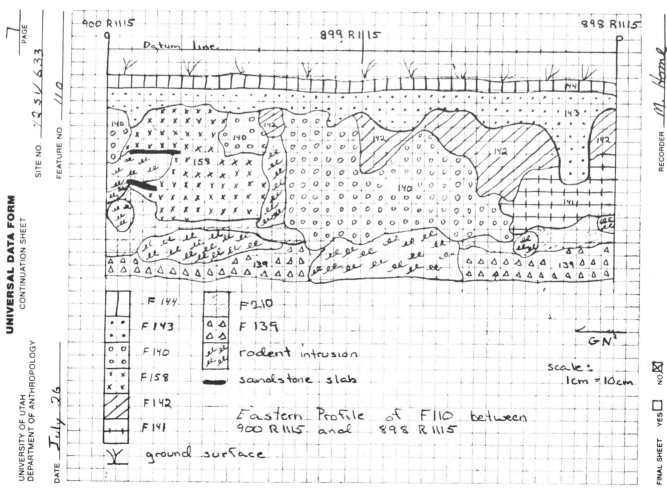

shelters as do people, for example. As a result, our ability to clearly define prehistoric groups such as those who occupied the northern Colorado Plateau and the eastern Great Basin is made even more difficult.

Part of our problem with understanding the Fremont has been this difficulty in, first, identifying and classifying these material remains, and, second and ultimately more importantly, determining how they relate to how and why people do what they do. Early archaeologists working in the region were faced with the almost overwhelming problem of determining the relationships of past remains in time and space, and so, until very recently, Fremont archaeology has been almost completely oriented towards the cataloging of artifacts. Because of the inherent variation among Fremont groups, this process of classifying and cataloging has made the Fremont culture something of an enigma ever since it was first defined in 1931 by Noel Morss.

Morss was a young Harvard anthropology student on his way to becoming an attorney when he first began his work along the Fremont River in southcentral Utah (after which he named his newly defined culture). This was a time when American archaeology had just begun to emerge as a discipline and Morss' work is an excellent example of how archaeology was practiced in its early years. Prior to the twentieth century, archaeology was largely a collecting hobby of the leisure class and no formal academic structure for its study existed. After the second decade of the twentieth century, archaeology began to be taught in a number of universities as part of anthropology programs, but was oriented more toward history than toward human behavior. Archaeology was "pre" history and the major purpose of archaeologists was description and classification. The job of Morss and many other archaeologists of his time was to determine how old the artifacts left by prehistoric peoples were and to define just how they were distributed through the countryside. Since determining time/space relationships still remains a basic component of archaeology, this descriptive approach is essentially what the general public views as the work of archaeology and archaeologists. Indiana Jones and other

Figure 18 Noel Morss

Figure 19 Archaeologists of the Claflin-Emerson expedition work at Rock House Ruin along Hill Creek, east-central Utah. The Anasazi-like masonry construction of this site and others like it along the tributaries of the Green River is one feature which led archaeologists to consider the Fremont a "Northern Periphery" of the Anasazi. (Photo: Peabody Museum, Harvard University)

Hollywood archaeologists are merely stereotypes of what most people think archaeologists do—find exotic artifacts, determine how old they are and catalog them in museums.

When archaeology is approached in this way, prehistoric peoples are defined by grouping artifacts and other remains into categories or "traits." Long lists of traits, such as projectile point types, pottery types, architectural features, basketry designs, etc., are compiled for different areas and times. These lists are then compared and contrasted, and based on the degree of similarities or differences between lists, sets of archaeological sites (sites are any place where the remains of human activities are found, and range from a scatter of a few chipped stone flakes to the remains of an ancient city) or even individual layers within sites are grouped into "cultures." This was essentially what Morss did in 1931 and it is what all Fremont archaeologists did for the next forty years.

Morss initially went to the Fremont River area in 1928 and 1929 as part of the Claflin-Emerson expedition, sponsored by the Peabody Museum at Harvard University, to explore local variations of prehistoric pueblo cultures in the central Colorado Plateau. To their surprise, expedition members found traits much like the cliff-dwelling Anasazi of Mesa Verde, Chaco Canyon and most of the Four-corners area, but "...which showed consistently a degree of divergence from corresponding features of [these] orthodox cultures (Morss 1931:iv)." The traits on the list Morss defined for the Fremont were, in other words, like the Anasazi in some respects, but different in others, and Morss defined the Fremont by comparing the trait list he compiled to a similar one for the Anasazi. This comparison to the Anasazi is basically the means through which the Fremont have been identified ever since, and an internally consistent and widely accepted definition of the Fremont has never been developed. Given the lack of elaborate ceremonial kivas, polychrome pottery, detailed basketry designs, and other hallmarks of "higher" social organizations, the Fremont have always been considered to be some sort of poor, out-back Anasazi described by terms like "Puebloan," "Puebloid," or "Northern Periphery" of the Anasazi.

This trait-list orientation remained unchanged well into the 1970s and the end product of the gradually improving Fremont archaeological research was simply that the lists were longer and more comprehensive. Archaeological recovery techniques have improved so much that virtually every charred seed or tiny flake on the floor of a prehistoric house can now be recovered and identified. Such details, unfortunately, do not always help improve our understanding. What tends to happen as more and more details are added to interpretations geared toward classification and description is that classes or categories get ever finer and narrower. This is exactly what happened

Figure 20 One of the most common chipped stone tools was a simple flake. The edge of an obsidian flake is sharper than a scalpel, and flakes were probably used for butchering. (top: 42Bo1 11102.13, bottom: 42Bo1 11120.5)

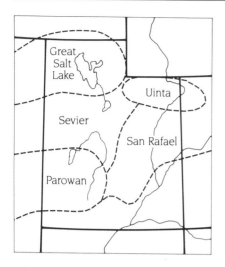

Figure 21 Fremont variants as defined by Jack Marwitt in 1970

with the Fremont. As more and more details became known about these people, they were grouped into increasingly larger numbers of "variants."

The most popular classification scheme was developed by Jack Marwitt in 1970. Marwitt defined five variants: the Uinta, Great Salt Lake, Sevier, San Rafael, and Parowan, but it is now clear that several more in northwestern Colorado, southern Idaho and eastern Nevada, could just as easily be defined. This trend toward defining more and more variants was almost inevitable given the degree of diversity characteristic of Fremont sites in general and the trait list approach used to define them. Unfortunately, it became increasingly apparent that trait lists specific enough to distinguish the Fremont from the Anasazi necessarily exclude one or more of the "variants," while lists general enough to include all the variants wind up grouping the Fremont and Anasazi together. As one Fremont archaeologist was "rather surprised" to note "...one of the principal difficulties in the use of trait lists to define the Fremont is the problem that there are actually rather few distinctive and typical traits that are found over the entire area usually considered to be Fremont (Ambler 1970:2)."

Archaeologists working on the Fremont in the 1970s reacted to this problem in a number of different ways. Many archaeologists added "ecological" analyses of the way people lived to existing artifact trait list definitions to try to understand how and why cultures change and adapt, and to define cultural variants in a more comprehensive fashion. They analyzed and defined Fremont sites in terms of their environmental settings and the ways that Fremont people used the plants and animals available to them. Unfortunately, the same diversity which plagued trait-list definitions of the Fremont made these environmentally defined variants equally fuzzy because environmental traits had merely been added to material traits in the definition of prehistoric "cultures." For example, in 1977, LaMar Lindsay and I identified three Fremont variants based principally on environmental settings and land-use patterns. In many ways they were similar to variants

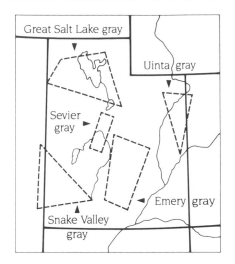

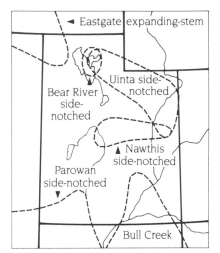

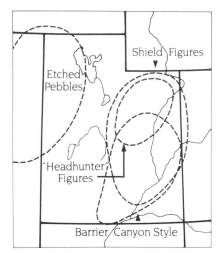

Figure 22 Distribution of several artifact traits often used to define the Fremont "Culture" and its variants (left to right: pottery types, projectile point styles, rock art styles)

defined through artifact trait-lists and proved to be just as unwieldy because of internal variability within each area. As a result, this and other ecological definitions of the Fremont were ultimately no more useful and no more widely accepted than the earlier artifact trait-list definitions.

Some archaeologists, and I am most definitely one, are now beginning to think that it is our concept of culture which is at the heart of our problem in defining the Fremont. Archaeologists have always tended to see culture as something tangible; something having boundaries and limits and which can be placed in categories. As a result they spent their time trying to identify the boundaries and limits of the Fremont culture and put it in an appropriate box. During my early work on the Fremont, this approach was the one I too favored, but recently I have started to see culture as something more elastic, a kind of unbounded social environment in which individuals find themselves. Just as each person is physically unique, so, too, each person is culturally unique. Each individual learns from a different set of other individuals and has a different way of living within the social environment. Despite these differences, people often act in a similar fashion; usually because doing so has greater social and economic rewards than does acting in other ways.

23

Figure 23 Pieces of broken pottery were used as scoops and possibly as scrapers in the construction of ceramic vessels. (42In40 1109.4)

It is possible to define such a set of common and widely shared behaviors as a "culture." In fact, the way in which anthropologists traditionally define a culture is to determine what is "normal" behavior; they define the average way of acting among a particular set of people. An anthropologist describing our culture, for example, might say one of our principal characteristics is that we watch television every night. This, of course, is true, most of us do. However, some of us do not—a few read, go for walks, or even attend museum-sponsored lectures. But such "abnormal" behavior is often ignored and, by defining cultures in terms of average behavior, anthropologists and archaeologists have tended to see cultures as more clearly bounded than they may actually be.

In short, a culture is simply a way of describing and integrating statistical summaries of individual actions, and, like any statistical sum, the range of variation can be small or great. What this means is that we cannot always expect to define clearly recognizable sets of traits that identify prehistoric "cultures," and that the problems Fremont archaeologists have had over the last half-century in trying to define the limits of the Fremont culture and its variants, may not be due to poor excavation techniques or to insufficient amounts of data, but to the fact that such limits do not exist. A prehistoric culture may be relatively broad and not easily defined for one set or sets of individuals such as the early pre-Fremont hunters and gatherers, or more easily bounded and readily identified among other groups, such as the Anasazi. Our problem with the Fremont is that they seem to lie towards the variable end of this scale.

One clear characteristic of the Fremont people was that they lived in many different kinds of environmental settings and were flexible enough to adapt to all of them. As a result, there was apparently a wide degree of variation in behavior and there is no one "set" of material remains resulting from that behavior which we can identify as Fremont. The Fremont seem to have ranged from full-time settled farmers to full-time mobile hunter-gatherers with everything in

24

between. This variation was not just regional, but also temporal, with village farmers growing corn, beans, and squash one year and breaking up into small bands of wandering wild plant collectors and hunters the next. Such variation is a problem when archaeologists try to put material remains in time and space categories, because it is almost impossible to pigeonhole such people. However, many archaeologists now see variation as an advantage when archaeology is done as anthropology, since it is the common aspects of this variation which allows us to understand why people act as they do. Many recent projects are geared less toward trying to define Fremont categories and more toward defining the many ways that people of the Fremont area were born, lived, reproduced and died. They are oriented toward understanding Fremont variation rather than Fremont variants and in telling us more about what it is to be human than in defining Fremont categories.

It is this orientation I hope to follow. I have not attempted to produce and describe sets of artifacts and sites in order to define the Fremont culture and its variants. I think that a better way of looking at the Fremont is to explore a sample of the many different kinds of sites and subsistence patterns which characterize Fremont flexibility and diversity.

Figure 24 Clay pipes were constructed in a variety of straight and elbow forms. (top: 42In40 fs1336.1, bottom: 42Jb2 fs591.5)

25

Rock art, Cockleburr Wash, Utah

The five sites or sets of sites described here are representative of the wide range of variation which characterizes the Fremont, but by no means do they cover the entire spectrum of how the Fremont lived. Variation and flexibility among the Fremont was so pronounced that a single individual may well have lived the entire range of variation,

FREMONT LIFEWAYS

from full-time farmer in a settled village to full-time mobile hunter-gatherer, in the space of a few years.

NAWTHIS VILLAGE

Nawthis village, a large farming community just east of Salina, Utah in the southern Wasatch Plateau, is representative of the classic sedentary villages occupied at the height of Fremont development around 1000 years ago. Life at these sites was supported by a combination of horticulture and the collection of local wild resources, with the relative proportions varying greatly depending on the local environmental setting. Individual lifestyles may have differed even within one of these villages, with some people, perhaps older individuals or those with very young children, staying primarily at the village tending crops, and others, perhaps families with older children or parties of young men, leaving the villages for extended collecting trips.

The setting at Nawthis is like many of the settled villages on either side of the Wasatch Plateau. It is located in a mixed pinyon-juniper

Figure 25 Ivie Creek black-on-white pottery, common to only a small part of the Fremont area along either side of the Wasatch Plateau in central Utah, is distinct from other varieties of Fremont pottery in having a white slip on which geometric designs have been painted. Ivie Creek black-on-white bowl (11281)

28

forest adjacent to Gooseberry Creek (a tributary of Salina Creek) at an elevation of 6600 feet. Open sagebrush and grass meadows are found on many areas of the floodplain, and cottonwoods, willows, service berries, and other streamside plants are found along the creek. Aspen and fir are found on the nearby mountain slopes just above the site and the people of Nawthis Village had ready access to the plants and animals common to higher elevations as well as to streamside habitats and valley bottom locations in the nearby Sevier River valley.

Nawthis may actually represent a series of sites, in that it is composed of more than thirty mounds scattered along the margin of

Figure 26 This view across Nawthis Village is typical of canyon mouth settings at the base of the pinyon juniper forest where most Fremont village sites along the Wasatch Plateau occur. (Photo: University of Utah Archaeological Center)

Figure 27 The single largest Fremont structure yet found is this multi-roomed mud-walled structure at Nawthis Village. It contains two rooms used principally for domestic purposes and another seven used for storage or access. (Photo: University of Utah Archaeological Center)

Figure 28 This circular pithouse structure at Median Village in the Parowan Valley north of Cedar City, Utah is characteristic of the houses found at large village sites along the western flanks of the Wasatch Plateau. (Photo: University of Utah Archaeological Center)

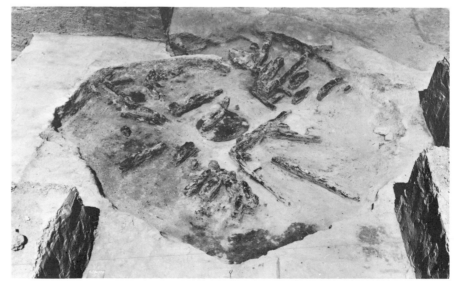

Figure 29 Single and double roomed mud-walled storage structures, such as these from Nawthis Village, are characteristic of Fremont village sites in the eastern Great Basin. (Photo: University of Utah Archaeological Center)

Gooseberry Creek. Since radiocarbon dates from the site span a period of three hundred to seven hundred years centering around 1000 years ago, it is probable that many of these mounds were occupied sequentially rather than simultaneously. This is a common pattern at other large "village" sites. At the nearby Five-Finger Ridge, for example, where Fremont Indian State Park is now located, over eighty structures are present and an extensive suite of radiocarbon dates suggests that only a few were occupied at any one time. These "villages" may actually have been occupied, abandoned, and re-occupied by relatively small groups of several interrelated families.

Only a small portion of Nawthis Village has been excavated, but even the limited number of architectural features exposed in three of the mounds suggests that differences within this site were as marked as those found between sites. Seven surface structures and five pit structures were identified. The surface structures were made principally of mud blocks, but one was made with basalt boulders. They vary in

Figure 30 Plan map diagram of the Old Woman Site along Ivie Creek in central Utah. This configuration of a small number of semi-subterranean houses and above ground mud-walled granaries is a common pattern for the hamlet villages along the eastern margin of the Wasatch Plateau. (Photo: University of Utah Archaeological Center)

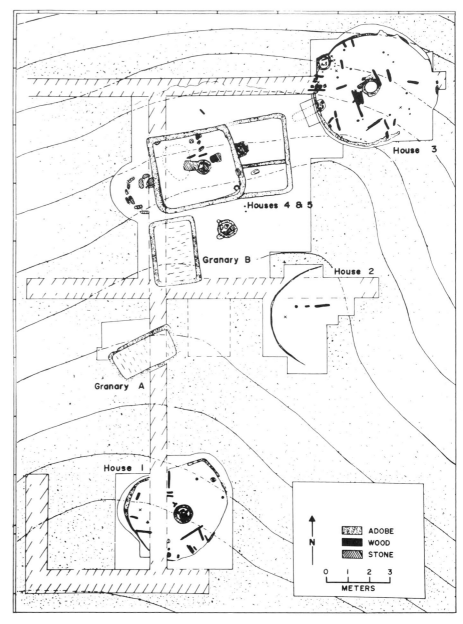

size from small (2 x 3m) one-room structures to a large (10 x 10m) nine-room structure. Most were used primarily for storage, but the presence of prepared firepits on the floors and numerous domestic artifacts such as grinding stones and bone tools suggests that some multi-room structures were apparently used for both residential and storage purposes. Walls are vertical (up to 1.7m high); shapes were rectangular to square; roofs appear to have been flat. Construction techniques used in the circular to sub-rectangular 5-7m diameter pit structures are equally varied. There are structures with unlined pit walls, with clay lined walls, with separate adobe and boulder walls constructed within a pit, and with adobe walls on the downhill side of a structure dug into a slope. Their common features are interior hearths and ventilator shafts.

Common artifacts include Sevier gray, Emery gray, and Ivie Creek black-on-white ceramics, Rose Springs, Nawthis, and Bull Creek projectile points, "Utah" type trough metates (metates with both primary and secondary grinding areas), and a bewildering variety of bone awls and weaving tools. People depended on a mix of domesticated plants and a wide array of wild resources for food. Twenty-six animal and twenty-five plant types, all of which are available locally today, were apparently used by the villagers. Some of the many wild plants include pinyon nuts, chenopod seeds, cattails, and Indian rice grass. Deer and mountain sheep were common large game, but rabbits, squirrels, and other smaller animals may have been the most common source of meat. Corn, beans, and squash were grown on nearby flood plains, probably using flood-water farming techniques. Nawthis is unique in having some evidence of the use of irrigation, but other large village sites may also have had some means of directing water to crops. Many village sites are located on alluvial fans just below the mouth of a nearby canyon where stream flows can be readily directed over small farm plots and it was probably easier to move the plot or even the entire village than it was to build large-scale irrigation features.

It appears that Nawthis was occupied year-round, and the above ground storage structures were apparently used to hold both harvested wild and domesticated plant crops through the winter months. However, in the cliffs along the nearby Salina Creek, a number of small pole and mud-walled storage granaries were constructed in small

Figure 31 For a long time stone balls commonly found at Fremont village sites were thought to be part of a game, but recent work suggests they may have been used with metates. (top to bottom: 42Un95 fs410.9, 42Un95 fs289.85, 42In124 fs158.86)

33

Figure 32 The secondary grinding platform on "Utah-type" metates may have been used in conjunction with the stone balls found at many Fremont sites. Metate and matching mano from Pharo Village (Utah Division of State History 42Md180)

Figure 33 Manos (the hand-held part of a grinding set) come in as many different varieties as metates (the fixed part). Mano forms include formed and unshaped, one-handed and two-handed, one-sided and two-sided, and flat and rocker shaped. They, like the different metates, were probably used to grind different kinds of seeds. (left to right: 42Dc48 fs11.4, 42Un126 fs87.1, 42Md180 fs335.1)

overhangs and crevices. They are all in locations that are difficult to reach and which cannot be readily seen by the casual observer, and it has been suggested that they may have served to cache seed corn and other important resources during periods when the village sites had to be abandoned. Many village sites like Nawthis are in areas that were marginal for aboriginal corn agriculture, and it is probable that crops failed at times and that local wild resources were insufficient to support the village population. During these periods, most of the village population, even older people and those with young children, may have switched to a more mobile hunting and gathering existence for a while, but left enough seed corn in hidden granaries to sow another crop upon their return.

In some areas, the growing season was long enough and water plentiful enough that crop failures were rare, while in others, nearby wild resources such as cattails, fish and other resources along rivers and lakes were productive enough that crop failures could be mitigated and villages may not have been completely abandoned. In yet

Figure 34 Large chipped and ground tools sometimes called hoes may also have been used as axes. Large trees were probably felled by a tedious and time consuming procedure in which a fire is built around the base, a layer of charred wood is removed with a stone axe, the fire is re-built, another layer is removed, and so on until the tree topples over. (16083)

Figure 35 Isolated stick and mud-walled storage granary in Salina Canyon, central Utah (Photo: University of Utah Archaeological Center)

others, everyone had to be ready to move and the threat of crop failure may have been very real and constant. With the coming long, cold Great Basin winter reflected in the eyes of their children, Fremont parents must often have had to make the difficult choice of whether to leave a crop in the field and go collect the wild foods which were often available for only a short time, or to ignore the wild plants and animals which could get them through the winter on the chance they might save the crop.

Figure 36 A basalt boulder-lined house structure at Windy Ridge Village is characteristic of house styles found along the eastern margin of the Wasatch Plateau. Earth pushed up around the outside of the rocks makes these houses very like the semi-subterranean structures found elsewhere, and may have been an adaptation to rocky terrain. Semi-subterranean houses are more energy efficient than are surface structures. (Photo: University of Utah Archaeological Center)

BULL CREEK   The dry and desolate plateau and canyon country north of the Colorado River differs in many ways from the flanks of the Great Basin/Plateau transition zone. While there are numerous permanent rivers, such as the Green, San Rafael, Dirty Devil, White, and Price, which flow through the region, the land between is poorly vegetated and the absence of numerous small snow-fed mountain streams makes the flood-water farming practiced by the Fremont a very risky business. As a result, Fremont village sites on most of the Colorado Plateau (the southern flanks of the Uinta Mountains are the exception) often consist of a series of small isolated sites located at great distances from each other.

Sites along Bull Creek on the northern flank of the Henry Mountains north of Lake Powell and the Colorado River, are representative of many of these smaller residential villages of the Colorado Plateau. They illustrate the difficulty archaeologists have in defining "cultures" on the basis of trait lists. Bull Creek lies in the dry badlands country between Hanksville, Utah and the foothills of the Henry Mountains and the only reliable water source is the creek itself. Vegetation consists primarily of small greasewood, grasses, and cacti, with some rare junipers in moister spots. Cottonwoods are found in

Figure 37 Snares and dead-fall traps were widely used for taking small game animals. A number were probably set in a trap line and there may have been dozens in a hunters's kit. For example, there are numerous individual snares in this set from the San Rafael Swell area of east central Utah. (42Em177 fs43.1)

Figure 38 Archaeologist's sketch of a feature at Hillside Cache, Bull Creek

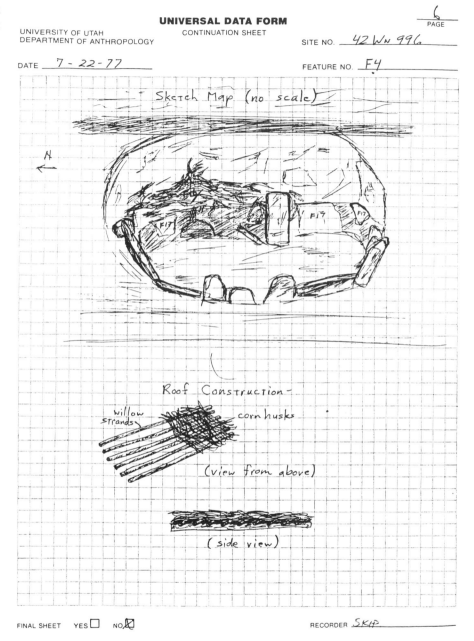

UNIVERSAL DATA FORM
CONTINUATION SHEET

UNIVERSITY OF UTAH
DEPARTMENT OF ANTHROPOLOGY

PAGE 6

SITE NO. 42 Wn 996

DATE 7-22-77

FEATURE NO. F4

Sketch Map (no scale)

N

F17   F17   F17

Roof Construction -

willow strands   corn husks

(view from above)

(side view)

FINAL SHEET   YES ☐   NO ☒   RECORDER SKIP

scattered clusters along the creek, but even streamside vegetation is limited. Animal life is limited to small game common to desert environments, but antelope may have been available prehistorically. Bison thrive in the Henry Mountains today, though the only large game identified in the Bull Creek sites were mountain sheep and antelope.

The many sites along Bull Creek (over one hundred were identified) apparently served a variety of purposes; permanent (or semi-permanent) dwellings, lithic quarries, storage areas, small temporary camps, rockshelters, and observation sites can be identified. The whole complex appears to have been occupied between about 800 to 1200 years ago by people utilizing a combination of domesticated resources and wild plants and animals. The habitation sites consist of small circular (4-6m dia.) pit houses with entry way/ventilator shafts and interior hearths. Some are rock-lined. No more than three structures occur at each site and they appear to have been occupied by only one or two families. A single rectangular rock-walled above-ground storage structure is usually associated with these pit structures.

The houses are very reminiscent of early Anasazi pit structures, and they contain features, such as slab-lined grinding bins, that are not

Figure 39 Large bifacially worked choppers may have been used for dismembering large game and for breaking up bones for marrow. (42In124 fs393.13)

Figure 40 Slab-lined storage cists and mealing bins characteristic of Anasazi sites to the south are found along Bull Creek. (Photo: University of Utah Archaeological Center)

Figure 41 A set of painted stick gaming pieces (42To13 AR948)

Figure 42 The necklaces shown on both clay figurines and rock art figures suggest that they were a common decorative item of Fremont peoples. Bone necklace (42In40 fs152.3)

Figure 43 Seven different types of projectile points have been defined for the Fremont. They were probably hafted on arrow foreshafts. Larger points may have served as knives or multi-purpose tools. (top to bottom: Uinta side-notched, 42Un95 fs151.1; Rose Spring corner-notched, 42Dc2 fs7.22; Bull Creek, 42Sv21 fs16; Eastgate expanding stem, 42Bo268 fs128.21; Bear River side-notched, 42Bo57 AR2113)

usually found in "Fremont" houses. Stone-lined storage cists, also characteristic of early Anasazi sites, are found along Bull Creek. Artifacts are unusual in that a mix of both "Anasazi" and "Fremont" styles are present. A number of different pottery types are present at each site, but at some, "Anasazi" types such as Moenkopi corrugated and Tusayan polychrome predominate, while at others "Fremont" types such as Emery gray are in the majority. Projectile points include both Parowan basal-notched and Nawthis side-notched points common in Fremont sites to the north and west, and Bull Creek points found in large numbers in Anasazi sites to the south. Grinding stones include both trough and slab types, but only two "Utah" type metates were recovered. The few identifiable basketry remains are "Fremont" types.

Given the wide array of architecture and artifacts at the Bull Creek sites, it would be very difficult to categorize them as either "Fremont" or "Anasazi" by using a trait list. The sites were initially called Fremont, primarily I think, because the archaeologists who excavated and reported them were Fremont specialists rather than Anasazi specialists. But if they cannot readily be classified as "Fremont" and they have too many Fremont features to be "Anasazi," then what are they? The problem becomes clearer at a site on the south side of the Henry Mountains. At Ticaboo, a burial of a young girl (excavated because of vandalism) contained "Fremont" moccasins, "Anasazi" pottery, and Bull Creek points found in both "Fremont" and "Anasazi" sites. So who was buried at Ticaboo? Was she Fremont or Anasazi? I prefer the easy solution. The girl buried at Ticaboo and the other people who occupied the Bull Creek complex and other Henry Mountain sites, were clearly "Freazi." Or were they "Anamonts?"

The Bull Creek sites are representative of sites on the Colorado Plateau as a whole. As one moves north along the Green River across the Colorado Plateau, "Anasazi" features diminish and more classic "Fremont" features are more common. Even so, the sites on the Colorado Plateau are, as a group, distinctive from Fremont sites in Great Basin drainages. They are generally smaller, containing less than five coursed and uncoursed masonry structures. "Village" sites in the Basin are generally larger and are characterized by adobe walled structures. Sites on the Plateau also have higher percentages of Anasazi "trade" items than do Basin sites.

Along the eastern margin of the Great Basin, the snow-fed rivers of the Wasatch and Uinta mountains find their final home in the closed-basin valleys of what was once Lake Bonneville. As this water spreads out across the relatively flat Ice Age lake bottoms, it creates a number of vast oases in the midst of comparatively harsh desert environments. These large saline marsh areas constitute some of the

ORBIT INN

Figure 44 In the marshes of the eastern Great Salt Lake, sites are located on the levees of distributary channels such as this one along the lower Bear River. (Photo: University of Utah Archaeological Center)

43

richest ecosystems within the Fremont region and the large array of fish, waterfowl, shellfish, and marsh plants found closely spaced within these marshes provided some Fremont groups with wild resources that were as productive and reliable as any domestic crop.

Orbit Inn and other sites along the Bear River are characteristic of a different kind of "village" life found in these large, rich marsh areas surrounding Utah and Great Salt Lakes. These sites represent two phases; one dating to about 500-1200 years ago and another dating about 300 to 500 years ago. The first of these phases corresponds to the classic Fremont period, while the latter is related to the "Late Prehistoric" period often thought to represent sites left by the immediate ancestors of historic Shoshoni and Ute people. The two phases are characterized, for the most part, by different kinds of artifacts, but some evidence of common subsistence practices have suggested to some archaeologists that the sites and the people who left them may be related.

Figure 45 The Fremont typically produced a wide array of bone tools, including a variety of awls. They may all have had specialized purposes ranging from use as punches to weaving and engraving tools. (top to bottom: 42Md180 fs179.274, 42Em47 AR1542, 42Sv5, 11037, 42Md180 fs81.3)

Figure 46 Many of the Great Salt Lake marsh sites, such as Bear River II, consist of surface arrangements of postholes and numerous small storage pits. (Photo: University of Utah Archaeological Center)

Figure 47 Mats made of cattails (*Typha* L.) or bulrush (*Scirpus* L.) are often found in sites with good preservation. They may have been used as sleeping mats. (42Bo1 9597)

45

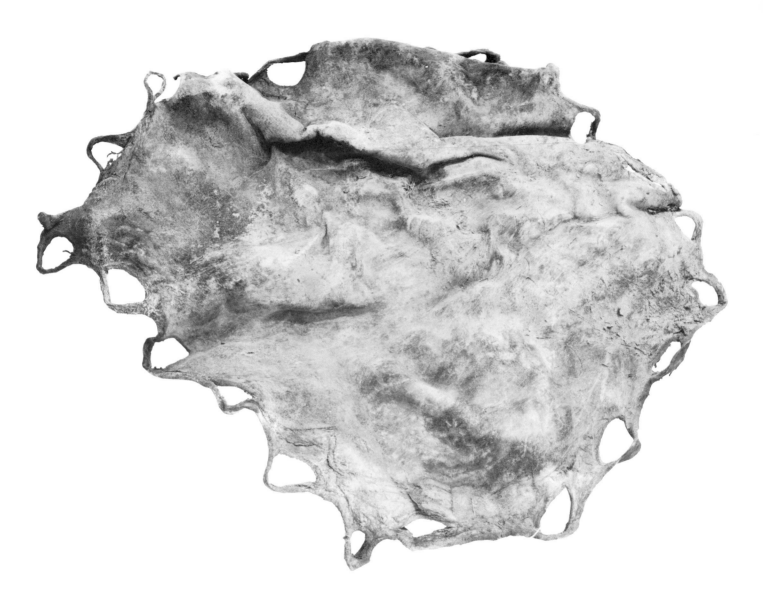

Figure 48 Hides were prepared by stretching and drying. Cut marks made by a stone scraper are clearly visible on the surface of this hide. (42Bo1 9625)

Figure 49 Shallow pit structures, necessitated by the high water table, are characteristic of the early phase around the Great Salt Lake. (Photo: University of Utah Archaeological Center)

Figure 50 Bone harpoon tips are found at Fremont sites along the streams and lakes of the Wasatch Front. (left to right: 42Bo57 21283; Brigham Young University, Museum of Peoples and Cultures, 72.29.64.1; 42Bo57 FS22.13)

The sites are located on deltas of the Bear, Ogden/Weber, and Jordan Rivers, where stream flows slow and the rivers break up into numerous meandering channels. The sites are built on natural levees which rise three to five feet above surrounding wetlands habitats. Site density in these marshes is as high or higher than any other region in Utah (including those occupied by the Anasazi) and it is almost impossible to distinguish one site from another along the length of the levees because they are so numerous. The favored site locations were apparently close to the edge of the lake, and as the lake rose and fell with changes in climate, sites were placed higher or lower on the relatively flat deltas. For example, most of the earlier Fremont sites are at elevations above 4210', while the Late Prehistoric sites are located down to 4205' and even lower. Marsh vegetation, such as sedges and bulrush dominate along the stream channels, and salt-loving grasses and pickleweed plants are found in drier areas. Waterfowl, muskrats and other marsh animals are common and bison were locally available prehistorically.

Figure 51 Fingernail impressions along the vessel rim or neck is a common decorative technique found in Late Prehistoric pottery; its presence on this Great Salt Lake gray jar is one of the few bits of material evidence supporting a connection between the Fremont and later peoples. (11212)

Figure 52 Slate knives with both ground and flaked edges are common in Fremont sites around the Great Salt Lake. (left to right: 42Bo57 fs253.2, 23652.47, 42Bo57 fs51.54)

Architecture was simple: shallow pit structures and light surface pole-and-brush huts or windbreaks. The pit structures do not occur in the later sites, but both styles are found in the earlier sites. Storage was limited to small pits often capped with clay, and no formal storage structures were constructed. Characteristic artifacts include coiled Great Salt Lake gray pottery during the Fremont period, and Brownware pottery, made by forming the clay between a paddle and hand held stone rather than with clay coils, during the Late Prehistoric phase. The Great Salt Lake Fremont, unlike the Fremont to the south, had no painted varieties of pottery. Promontory gray, a thick-walled pottery resembling the Brownwares made later by Numic people is

49

found on the earlier Fremont sites. Its presence suggests to some archaeologists that Fremont and Late Prehistoric groups are related, but it may also simply be the result of a later occupation of the same sites; and the relationship between the two phases remains unresolved. Other artifacts include corner-notched arrow points in the early phase and side-notched points in the later phase. Sleek polished slate knives and heavy stone pestles are unique to the area. A variety of bone tools and chipped stone side scrapers were also used.

During both periods, people depended on a wide array of marsh plants including bulrush, cattails, mustard, chenopods, plantago and marsh grasses. Common animal resources include fish (probably caught in traps along the rivers), ducks and other shorebirds, muskrats, and fresh-water mollusks. Bison bones are also quite common in these sites. Most of these resources were collected seasonally, principally in the spring and again in the fall and it is probable that the later sites, such as Orbit Inn, were only occupied periodically throughout the year.

While the earlier Bear River sites also suggest periodic occupation, historic accounts by trappers like Peter Skene Ogden speak of people living in the general marsh area at all seasons of the year. This seemingly contradictory evidence forces us to re-think our commonly held ideas about sedentary versus mobile settlement strategies. These groups were certainly mobile, but within a limited area; moving

Figure 53 Bone whistles are frequently found at Fremont sites. (top to bottom: 42Bo55 fs50.34, 42Un95 fs296.37, 42Un95 fs2.10)

upstream to collect fish during spawning runs and out to the edges of the deltas to collect bulrush seeds when they ripened. Some people may not have moved at all, while other people may have moved a number of times in any one year. During the earlier Fremont phase, this limited movement may have been associated with farming at sites higher on nearby alluvial fans. At Willard, Utah, for example, Fremont sites where people were growing corn and storing it in mud-walled granaries are located less than a mile from Fremont sites in the marshes where people were collecting bulrush seeds and hunting ducks. People also took longer trips to collect pine nuts or to hunt mountain sheep or elk. Some of these trips may have been to the numerous cave sites on the western margin of the Great Salt Lake.

The fault-block mountains and valleys of the east-central Great Basin create a landscape of contrasts. The salt and mud of dry lake bottoms give way to low sagebrush and saltbush covered alluvial fans and eventually to juniper and pinyon on the upper mountain slopes. Aspen and firs are found in limited areas on only a few of the largest ranges; permanent streams are equally rare. Available water is limited, and in many areas the small spring-fed marshes found along many of the faults at the base of isolated mountain ranges constituted the only concentrated areas of resources available to prehistoric peoples. Caves and rockshelters near these springs contain some of the best evidence of how Fremont groups lived in this desert environment.

Deeply layered dry cave sites like Hogup and Danger Caves, found around the rim of the Great Salt Lake Desert, are useful in interpreting Fremont groups in several important ways. First, deposits at the sites represent repeated visits by hunting and gathering groups from more than 10,000 years ago to less than fifty years ago, and the layer-by-layer excavation of these sites, as opposed to excavation of the relatively short chronological "windows" available at most open village sites, allows us to see the Fremont in relation to more ancient hunting and gathering peoples. Second, the sites clearly represent the more

HOGUP CAVE

Figure 54 Horned figurine from Hogup Cave (42Bo36 fs125.70; Photo: University of Utah Archaeological Center)

51

Figure 55 The view from the mouth of Hogup Cave looking across the playas of the Great Salt Lake Desert toward the Newfoundland Mountains is typical of that seen from many caves in the western Utah deserts. (Photo: University of Utah Archaeological Center)

mobile end of a wide range of subsistence/settlement patterns, and the interpretation of the Fremont deposits at Hogup Cave and sites like it provides a useful comparison to sites like Nawthis Village. Third, preservation at these dry enclosed sites is excellent and most of the evidence we have of the many perishable artifacts such as rabbitskin robes, baskets, moccasins, nets, digging sticks, and any number of other tools, is derived from these sites.

Hogup and Danger Caves are both large caverns produced by the waves of Lake Bonneville working on the limestone cliffs of eastern

52

Great Basin mountains. They overlook the salt flats of the western Utah deserts, but both are associated with small springs and the marsh plants and animals these springs support. The caves are well below the pinyon-juniper belt and the mountain slopes in which they lie are dominated by low sagebrush and saltbush. Along the margins of the salt flats, salt-tolerant plants like pickleweed produce large, but difficult to collect, quantities of small seeds. The caves are more than one hundred miles from the nearest known village site, making transportation of food stuffs and other resources between sites difficult.

Figure 56 These horned figurines from the Fremont levels at Hogup Cave are constructed of bone, wood, plant materials, and occasionally feathers. (top to bottom, both 42Bo36: fs48.575(c), fs47.117, Photo: University of Utah Archaeological Center)

Figure 57 Profile of Hogup Cave showing the thin layers of pickleweed chaff, antelope hair, saltbush twigs and other remnants of periodic visits to the cave (Photo: University of Utah Archaeological Center)

53

Many of the traits that characterize the Fremont are present in these cave deposits well before the appearance of pottery and corn. Small corner-notched projectile points, one-rod-and-bundle coiled basketry, and leather footgear are all present by about 2500 years ago. Dating problems at Hogup and Danger Caves make it difficult to pinpoint when pottery, and corn were introduced, and there is a possibility that a major occupation break occurred around 2000 years ago, but it is clear that by about 1300 years ago, all the classic Fremont elements (with the exception of clay figurines) are present at the two sites. By 800-900 years ago, artifacts such as Brownware pottery characteristic of the Late Prehistoric groups begin to occur in the same depositional layers with Fremont materials, but by 600-700 years ago all characteristic Fremont traits disappear from the record.

Figure 58 Winter clothing probably consisted of robes made of twisted rabbit skin. Occasionally, feathers were twisted into the robe. Elk and buffalo hide robes were probably also worn. Rabbitskin robe (42Em177 fs82.1; Photo: University of Utah Archaeological Center)

Figure 59 Etched stone artifacts, such as these examples of portable rock art from the Fremont levels of Hogup Cave, are common in caves around the Great Salt Lake and in the central Great Basin. (left to right, all 42Bo36: fs86.72, fs 429.222, fs184.44, fs114.45)

This overlap is interesting because it argues for the appearance of a new group of people in the area. A more transitional change in artifacts styles would be expected if the same group of people gradually, over time, modified their subsistence strategies and the tools that went with them.

The numerous caves and rockshelters in the limestone mountains of the eastern Great Basin provided natural shelters and storage facilities for the mobile hunter-gatherers who inhabited the region. The caves undoubtedly functioned in a number of different ways depending on the environmental setting in which they were found. Some, like Hogup, Danger and Fish Springs Caves were probably the focus of late fall and winter occupation. Most of these sites are associated with spring-fed marshes. Resources, such as bulrush rhizomes, available in the winter, supplemented stored food collected in the summer and early fall. Others, such as Lakeside and Floating Island Caves, were the focus of short-term visits associated with the collection of particular food resources (people came to collect grasshoppers in the case of Lakeside and pickleweed seeds in the case of Floating Island).

The subsistence patterns represented at each site differ with the setting, as might be expected, but what is perhaps most surprising is that the time of year people lived at the sites and what they did while

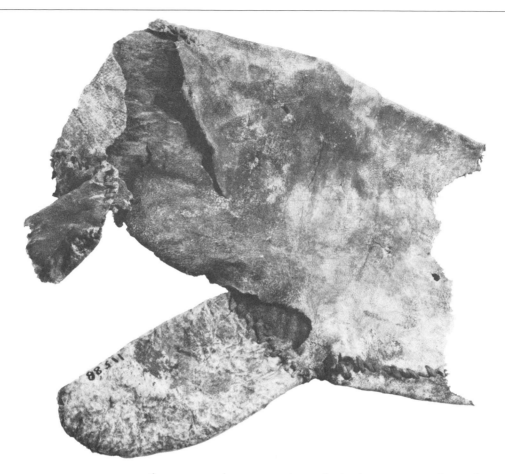

they were there remains relatively constant through time. For example, throughout the use of Hogup by early hunter-gathering, Fremont, and Late Prehistoric people, pickleweed collecting and antelope/rabbit hunting seem to have been the primary activities. Fluctuations occur in the number of deer, marsh birds and other plants which were collected, but the basic way of life does not change. This suggests that not only did the local habitat remain relatively stable over the last ten thousand years, but the way the site was used within the over-all yearly pattern of food collecting, did not change significantly over time. Domesticates, such as corn, are present in the Fremont levels at these cave sites, suggesting the possibility that these deposits represent occupation by part-time hunters and gatherers who either left their villages and crops for part of the year or else alternated between farming and collecting wild resources on a yearly or multi-year basis. Domesticates are rare, however, and the continuity of subsistence patterns suggest the possibility that these people may have been full-time hunter-gatherers who traded with settled villagers for corn and perhaps pottery and other artifacts. At present, it is not possible to reject either of these possibilities.

Many distinctive artifacts in the Fremont levels at Hogup and Danger Caves, such as Great Salt Lake gray pottery and corner-notched arrow points, are similar to those found at sites around the Great Salt Lake. Many others, however, particularly the perishable artifacts, are unique to these dry caves and their excavation has contributed greatly to our understanding of material remains left by the Fremont. These deposits contain netting for use in rabbit nets, twine for binding and snare traps, distinctive Fremont-type moccasins, one-rod-and-bundle basketry, "horned" figurines made of wrapped plant fiber, arrows and bow parts, rabbit skin robes and other clothing, leather pouches, numerous kinds of bone and shell beads (some traded from coastal areas), and much more. What these sites show is that the Fremont had a remarkably complex technological system involving many different types of food collecting tools, storage and transport gear, clothing and decorative items, and a wide variety of other materials.

Pithouse villages, deeply stratified caves and densely packed site locations all suggest rather stable life-styles for many Fremont peoples. However, most Fremont sites actually consist of small camp-sites scattered throughout many habitats ranging from grass covered sand dunes in valley bottoms to the pygmy forests of pinyon and juniper. Virtually every ecosystem in the Great Basin/Colorado Plateau region was utilized and it is difficult to single-out a representative site from the many locations occupied only briefly at different times of the year for different purposes.

Figure 61 Beads were made from a variety of materials: bone, shell, ceramic and stone, including lignite, azurite and turquoise. (top, left to right: 42Bo57 fs349.8, 42Md180 fs252.71, 42Bo268 fs124.3, bottom, left to right: 42Jb2 fs773.1, 42Wb34 fs 335.2, 42Sv5 AR1749)

TOPAZ SLOUGH

Figure 62 The low sand dunes at Topaz Slough may have helped protect temporary wind-break structures, and also provided resources such as Indian rice grass. (Photo: University of Utah Archaeological Center)

The many cave and marsh sites around the Great Salt Lake indicate that many Fremont people were mobile, but it is the small, temporary open sites such as Topaz Slough in the Sevier Desert that most strongly suggest that at least some Fremont were full-time hunter-gatherers. Topaz Slough and other nearby sites are found in the small dunes near old river channels that support wetland/marsh resources during periods of high water. Shadscale, saltbush, and greasewood dominate on alkali flats, while bunchgrass and Indian ricegrass are found on the dunes. Rabbits, small rodents, insects, lizards and an occasional antelope are the most available sources of animal protein.

At Topaz Slough, artifact concentrations of firecracked rock, chipped stone flaking debris and projectile points, grinding stones, and Fremont ceramics occur in areas exposed by dune erosion. Two structures and a refuse area are associated with these artifact concentrations. The only excavated structure dates to about 900 years ago and consists of a 2-3m shallow depression scooped out of the sand dune and covered with a brush pole structure. The structure was made of

Figure 63 Thin, small, and, most importantly light, slab-type metates are often found at temporary sites, and were probably part of the food processing equipment carried by mobile Fremont groups. (Utah Division of State History 42To106 fs347)

Figure 64 Brush structures, much like this Southern Paiute house photographed in 1873 by John K. Hilliers, are characteristic of structures found at Topaz Slough and other temporary sites. (Photo: Smithsonian Institution, National Anthropological Archives)

greasewood and saltbush on a willow or cottonwood pole frame and appears to have been roofed. A small hearth was found inside. Altogether, the structure resembles a wickiup used by historically known hunter-gatherers of the desert West. However, those built during the warmer months were often open on one side, were rarely roofed, and usually did not contain interior hearths, suggesting that this "temporary" structure may have been used in the late fall or winter.

It is difficult to determine what foods the occupants of Topaz Slough depended on. A variety of wild plant seeds, particularly chenopods, were recovered by archaeologists, but they may have been naturally introduced by the wind or by rodents. Bones of jackrabbits and snakes were common but, again, we cannot be sure that people brought them. However, the alkalinity of the surrounding terrain and the temporary nature of the structure itself, suggest that horticulture was not practiced locally and that these remains do represent a temporarily occupied camp where wild foods were collected. A single corn cob was found in the refuse area near the structure, but it seems likely it was acquired from farmers through some kind of exchange or was brought to the site by farmers who temporarily abandoned their fields.

Topaz Slough, like the dry caves to the north, probably represents one of the many facets of the more mobile Fremont groups. Whether it was occupied by full-time hunter-gatherers involved in a trading system with resident farmers, farmers supplementing their crops through a short-term collecting trip, or people who had abandoned farming for an extended period until the return of better conditions, is not yet known. Clearly however, it does suggest that mobility and the collection of wild resources were important aspects of the Fremont lifeway.

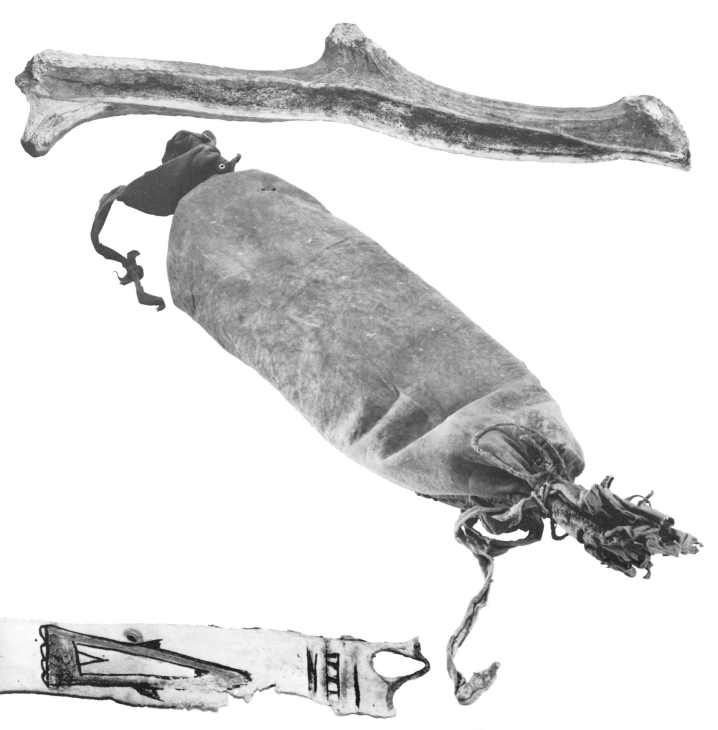

Rock art, Nine Mile Canyon, Utah

The key to understanding the Fremont is variation. A thousand years ago they ranged from settled farmers growing crops of corn and beans along the snow-fed streams of the larger mountain ranges to nomadic desert hunters and gatherers living on such wild foods as pine nuts and bulrush seeds, crickets and mountain sheep. These

REPRISE

63

Figure 66 Large, thin, bifacially worked chipped stone blades are a characteristic Fremont tool type. These blades are usually square bottomed, but were sometimes notched for easier hafting on short wooden handles. They were probably used as knives. (both: Utah Division of State History 42Ga2677)

patterns were not fixed; a single individual, within his or her lifetime, may, as environmental and social conditions changed, have lived at sites like all of those just described.

In many ways the Fremont were like the Anasazi to the south, but they had smaller and less densely populated villages and they were less organized, less integrated and more flexible. There are many traits which distinguish the Anasazi, but few artifacts characterize the Fremont as a whole, and even those that do, such as clay figurines, one-rod-and-bundle basketry, coil-made pottery, and moccasins, are not always found together. Etched stone tablets rather than clay figurines are usually found with pottery and basketry in the caves and rockshelters of the eastern Great Basin, for example. Architecture was varied; stone construction was favored in the east, while mud bricks were common in the west. Different projectile point styles were found throughout the Fremont area.

Such variation was probably part of an earlier long-standing pattern and southwestern traits such as pottery and farming were adopted in different ways about 2000 years ago by small groups of hunters and gatherers. By 500 years ago the Fremont were gone, but the end was probably as diverse as the beginning. After about 650 years ago the Anasazi world contracted to areas where modern Pueblos are now found, and the Fremont of the Colorado River drainages may have been part of this general pattern of withdrawal. In the eastern Great Basin, the Fremont may have been integrated into expanding Southern Paiute, Ute, and Shoshone populations. This integration may not have been entirely harmonious, and many Fremont groups may have died out.

Given this variability and diversity, what can we conclude about the Fremont? Above all they were people. They laughed, lusted, and lied. They were diligent and they were lazy. They fought, feasted, and feared the unknown. They worked and they played and raised as many children as they could. They were people, and by understanding them we can begin to understand ourselves.

Figure 67 Snake Valley corrugated vessel from Millard County (1714)

Figure 68 Some stone balls, such as this highly polished specimen from the Old Woman site, suggest a use other than as a grinding tool. (42Sv7 fs77)

We are only now beginning to see the Fremont as people. We know something of the what, and when, but only a little of the how and why. Many questions remain. Thirty years ago, James Gunnerson, a well-known Fremont archaeologist of the time, attempted to define the internal dimensions and external relationship of the Fremont (Colorado Plateau) and Sevier (Great Basin) cultures. Gunnerson (1960:373) suggested that "the Fremont is still not really well known, but there is already ample evidence of great variation in Fremont ceramics, architecture, and stonework. Fremont may be said to be characterized by experimentation and variability...there are, however generalized patterns and specific traits which occur consistently from site to site." More detailed work in the last three decades has confirmed all but the last portion of Gunnerson's statement. While the Fremont are still not known in detail and are still characterized by variability, the traits Gunnerson thought occurred consistently from site to site, are apparently not as consistent as he suggested.

Gunnerson thought settled life in small villages, an economy based on corn, bean and squash agriculture, pottery and a homogeneous art style characterized by elaborate human figures, were traits which could be consistently used to identify the Fremont. This remains true in some areas at some times, but we now know that small nomadic groups of people who collected wild plants and animals and lived in caves and small temporary brush structures also wore "Fremont" moccasins, used "Fremont" pottery, and made "Fremont" basketry.

This is a problem if we have a need to put this wide array of people and life-styles into boxes with labels on them. And, make no mistake, we often have such needs; just ask any museum curator if they can run a museum without boxes and labels. Better yet, ask yourself, as a museum visitor, if you feel more comfortable with or without everything categorized and explained. Yet, if we see the term "Fremont" as an umbrella which includes a diversity of human behavior, it becomes much easier to visualize these people of the eastern Great Basin and western Colorado Plateau as they actually were. They were essentially small groups of highly adaptable people living in an environmentally varied landscape. The problems that each of these groups had to deal with differed in smaller or larger ways, and the solutions each group arrived at and the tools each group used to achieve them also differed in smaller and larger ways. One set of individuals may have fared better as farmers, while another may have been more successful as hunters and plant collectors. In some ways these groups were very similar and in others very different. They may even have had different languages and different beliefs. Despite such diversity, or rather because of it, the Fremont are characterized by those most human of traits: adaptability.

During the fifteen hundred years that the Fremont can be distinguished, they produced an archaeological record as rich, yet as enigmatic, as any in the world. The record of how they lived, reacted and

Figure 69 The extensive working and polish on this bone effigy tool from Backhoe Village, central Utah, indicate it was used for weaving. Markings suggest it may also have been used for counting or record-keeping. (42Sv662)

responded to the changing world around them, is a mirror of ourselves; all peoples at all times and in all places. It is a record of human behavior. It is a record that is difficult to interpret and difficult to understand. But if we can clarify who and what the Fremont were, we will better understand how and why we act as we do, and what it means to be human in arid country. By exploring the Fremont, we explore ourselves as a people intrinsically tied to these desert lands.

Figure 70 Clay figurine from the Old Woman site (42Sv7 AR204)

Aikens, C. Melvin

1966 Fremont-Promontory-Plains Relationships. *University of Utah Anthropological Papers*, Number 82.

1970 Hogup Cave. *University of Utah Anthropological Papers*, Number 93.

Ambler, Richard

1970 Just what is Fremont? Paper presented at the XXXV Annual Meeting of the Society for American Archaeology, Mexico City.

Castleton, Kenneth B.

1979 *Petroglyphs and Pictographs of Utah*, Volumes One and Two. Utah Museum of Natural History.

Gunnerson, James H.

1960 The Fremont Culture: Internal Dimensions and External Relationships. *American Antiquity*, Volume 25, pp. 373-380.

1969 The Fremont Culture: A Study in Culture Dynamics on the Northern Anasazi Frontier. *Papers of the Peabody Museum of Archaeology and Ethnology, Harvard University*, Volume 59, Number Two.

Jennings, Jesse D.

1978 Prehistory of Utah and the Eastern Great Basin. *University of Utah Anthropological papers*, Number 98.

Jennings, Jesse D. and Dorothy Sammon-Lohse

1981 Bull Creek. *University of Utah Anthropological Papers*, Number 105.

Marwitt, John P.

1970 Median Village and Fremont Culture Regional Variation. *University Utah Anthropological Papers*, Number 95.

1986 Fremont Cultures. In, W. D'Azevedo (ed.), *Handbook of North American Indians, Volume 11, Great Basin*. pp. 161-172.

ADDITIONAL READING ON THE FREMONT

Madsen, David B.

1979 The Fremont and the Sevier: defining prehistoric agriculturalists north of the Anasazi. *American Antiquity*, Volume 44, pp. 711-723.

1980 Fremont Perspectives. *Antiquities Section Selected Papers*, Volume 7.

Madsen, David B. and James F. O'Connell

1982 *Man and Environment in the Great Basin*. Society for American Archaeology.

Morss, Noel

1931 The Ancient Culture of the Fremont River in Utah. *Papers of the Peabody Museum of American Archaeology and Ethnology, Harvard University*, Volume 12, Number 3.

Schaafsma, Polly

1971 The Rock Art of Utah. *Papers of the Peabody Museum of Archaeology and Ethnology, Harvard University*, Number 65.

Simms, Steven R.

1986 New Evidence for Fremont Adaptive Diversity. *Journal of California and Great Basin Anthropology*, volume 8, Number 2, pp. 204-216.

Wormington, H. M.

1955 A Reappraisal of the Fremont Culture. *Denver Museum of Natural History Proceedings*, Number One.